Praise for
Ugh!?! Not Another Diversity Book! (Workbook)

"Very high energy book, easy ideas to incorporate with very basic ideas presented in a new and exciting way. Recommend starting a "D.A.P." program at other universities."

"Very impressive, a talented, passionate and dedicated student affairs leader with wonderful ideas and sincerity."

"Excellent book! Interactive & well organized and the enthusiasm was contagious."

"The book is all that! Our first year students read it for their orientation readings!"

"Very inspiring, a gifted soul the author has to be to create a piece like this!"

Ugh!?! Not Another Diversity Book!(Workbook)

"When Multicultural Competence Meets A Real Reality."

Written By: Justin LaKyle Brown

Acknowledgement

First and foremost, let me say this…God has blessed me with many gifts and talents, and writing is certainly not one of them. I had to verbally record this book, have it transcribed, and then have it translated into text. Talk about a long process, right? Unfortunately for me, writing is one of my weaknesses but I believe that weaknesses are just excuses, so I continued to press forward.

The problem with acknowledging individuals or even writing an acknowledgement page is that I'm sure that I will omit someone. This isn't done intentionally, however, it is just the fact that there have been so many inspirational and influential people in my life. Please charge it to my head and not my heart.

A special thanks is extended to those who read portions of this book for clarity, content, and understanding. I appreciate you taking time out of your busy lives to assist me. Jeenal Shah and Kimberly Robinson. I could not have done this book without you. Thank you so much for all of your attention to detail, suggestions and ideas.

Ugh!?! Not Another Diversity Book Curriculum

This curriculum created from the _Ugh!?! Not Another Diversity Book_ is a straightforward curriculum that addresses real-world problems of diversity in today's society or on a college campus. Created for any classroom, any level of education as well as for the cultural diversity professional or the person who would simply like to learn more about the subject. The thought provoking questions alone will challenge your opinions and open your mind to review your own prejudices. Great for introducing the topic of diversity in classrooms, workshops, or debates. Thank you for purchasing and please share your feedback and experience.

Chapter 1...The Beginning

Goal – SWBAT Describe what 'Diversity' means to them individually.

Objective – Students will write a paragraph describing their own experiences with diversity.

Assessment –

1. Describe in your own words what diversity means to you.

2. Aside from skin color/ethnicity, what other elements of diversity encompass this umbrella term? (i.e. sexual orientation, religion, disability, etc.)

3. Thinking back to all the experiences you have had in your life, what aspects of diversity affect you the most?

4. Make of list of things in your life that define who you are as an individual. (i.e. hobbies, favorite foods, etc.) Discuss with your neighbors and see what everyone has in common and what makes everyone different.

5. What kind of community did you grow up in as a child? (i.e. low income, middle class, diverse, etc.)

6. In what ways did the community you were raised in influence your views on diversity?

7. Looking back on your past experiences, describe your first encounter with diversity. Was it positive? Was it negative? Explain.

8. What are your thoughts on Brown's experience at the mall of being racially profiled as a teenager?

9. Have you ever been in a situation where you were racially profiled? If not, do you know someone in your life who has been racially profiled? Explain the situation and how it made you feel.

10. Reflect on Mr. Morton words, "You're as good as you think you are." What do you think this means? In your own words, rephrase this quote in the way you interpreted it.

11. When in your life have you felt that you were not good enough for something?

12. Have you been in situation where you have felt out of place because of the color of your skin? If so, explain. How did it make you feel? If not, do you know anyone who this has happened to?

13. How would you characterize the frequency with which you encounter diversity in your life? Circle one.

    a. Never

    b. Sometimes

    c. Often

    d. Daily

14. What are some preconceived notions you have had about a particular group of people?

15. Why do you think it is important to be educated on multiculturalism and cultural awareness?

Chapter 2...This or That

Goal – SWBAT express their views about varied topics on diversity through a game called "This or That."

Objective – Students will come together and discuss their feelings and experience playing the game This or That.

Assessment–

1. Give some easy examples of categories for the game "This or that." (i.e. Cats or Dogs)

2. Give some more controversial examples of categories for the game "This or That." (i.e. Love or Money, Church or No Church)

3. Why do you think that for the more controversial topics in this game, like love or money, people's answers are not as simple as they are for cats or dogs?

4. Write a list of some reasons as to why people would choose money over love, either from the book or from your own experiences.

5. Switching perspectives, write a list of some reasons for why people would choose love over money, either from the book or from your own experiences.

6. Create groups of 4 people. Choose a topic from someone's list from question 2. Have people from both sides discuss their reasoning for being on that particular side. Then, take the perspective that you didn't argue for the first time to try and understand a different viewpoint. Give reasons for being in this viewpoint.

7. Reflect on the Privilege or No Privilege topic. In your own words, explain what you think both sides of this topic mean.

8. Brown brings up the idea of "black or white." Look back on an experience in your life that was not so black and white. How did it make you feel? How does this relate to the other ideas Brown brings in about the gray area between the black and white?

9. What is something you thought to be true because your parents told you it was true but as you grew up you began to form an opinion that was different than what you were taught?

10. Write about a situation where you experienced prejudice against something or someone. How did you feel? Did you realize at the time that this was prejudice?

11. Brown discusses how, even as babies', society places us in these boxes, like females having a pink room and males having a blue room. Give some examples of other ways society places us in a box based on our sex at birth.

12. The last paragraph of this chapter briefly mentions the political climate of the U.S. in 2017 with an example. Using your knowledge of current events, discuss another example that is similar to the one Brown discusses. If you cannot think of an example, use your own knowledge of U.S. history and relate it to a similar historical event.

Activity – Play 'This or That' Game.

Chapter 3...Stereotypes the New Phenomenon

Goal – SWBAT describe in their own words if they feel the "mass media" shapes their view of people, in terms of stereotypes.

Objective – Students will discuss if they represent the 'stereotypical view' of their race.

Assessment –

1. Brown jumpstarts this chapter with discussing mass media as an agent that shapes the way we view people. Think about his three examples of mass shootings. Name three different current events in which these labels were placed on the people who committed these shootings based on their skin color. If you cannot think of an example, use the internet as a resource.

2. Following the progression of this chapter, checkmark the box to in which you feel is the frequency with which you encounter people who fall within the indicated category.

	Never	Once	Sometimes	Often	Daily
Nerd					
Black Male					
Black Female					
Arab Male					
Feminist					
White Woman					
Handicap					
LGBTQIA					
Veteran					
White Male					

3. Do you think that the answers to the chart in question 2 affect the way you think and act towards people who fall in these categories? If so, explain. If not, explain.

4. Define feminism in your own words.

5. Why do you think that people who do not fall into the dichotomy or "box" that Brown brings up are viewed as "other" or "weird?" Why do you think people feel uncomfortable with people who do not conform to their own views?

6. "Identity is a reflexive process." What do you think Brown means by this? What do you take it to mean?

7. Get into groups and talk about people with disabilities. Are you a person with a disability? If so, discuss how this affects your life. If not, do you know someone who has a disability? Discuss how this affects your perceptions of people with disabilities.

8. Brown talks about people who use certain words or phrases without understanding the impact that those words have. (i.e. "no-homo", "that's so retarded", "queer", "rape", etc.) Can you think of other phrases or words people say that have similar negative unintended consequences? Why is not okay to say these things?

9. Circling back to the beginning of the chapter when Brown discusses media, how do you think the media affects the way we perceive veterans?

10. Why is the term "American Dream" tied to being white?

11. "Stereotypes are based on a kernel of truth." Explain this.

Activity – Students will play Stereotypes Charades and discuss what they learned from this activity about how they view stereotypes.

Chapter 4...Is That White Privilege I'm Smelling?

Goal – SWBAT define in their own words what the term 'White Privilege' means.

Objective – Students will come to understand how they perceive the word 'privilege' and how it affects them and additionally, how they use the term.

Assessment –

1. Based on your own experiences and what you have learned, describe white privilege in your own words.

2. After reading Brown's Mario Kart analogy, think about equality vs equity. (If you are unsure about what this is, use the internet as a resource.) How does the Mario Kart analogy connect to the idea of equality vs equity?

3. Compare and Contrast *Cross the Line* and Brown's anonymous questionnaire. Then, create a pro and con list for each activity. Why is it important to keep people's experiences anonymous?

Cross the Line | | Anonymous Questionnaire |

Pro	Con	Pro	Con

4. Why do you think it's important to have people of all different backgrounds in the workplace?

5. Look back at the history of the U.S. or even the world. What are some events that occurred in the past that might cause certain groups of people to feel transgenerational trauma?

6. What are microaggressions? Give some examples. Have you ever been a victim of a microaggression? If not, have you ever knowingly committed a microaggression?

7. Why is it important for children growing up to see people like themselves with successful careers? (i.e. professors, CEOs, engineers, businessmen, doctors, lawyers, etc.)

8. What is cultural appropriation? Aside from the ones Brown stated, give some examples of cultural appropriation. Why do you think cultural appropriation is a problem?

9. Define intersectionality. How does intersectionality play a role in your own life?

10. Do you experience any type of privilege? If so, what is it and why is it considered privilege?

11. "At one point in time, the world's best rapper was white, the world's best golfer was Black, and the tallest man in the NBA was Asian." Think about another example either in your life or in the media where people broke out of their stereotypes and explain the significance.

12. Look back on Brown's experience when his interviewer made assumptions about him solely based on his voice. When has someone assumed something about you that was incorrect? Was it positive or negative? How did it make you feel?

13. What are some ways that people with privilege can use their privilege in a positive way?

Activity – In a whole group discussion, students will discuss the privileges and disadvantages of their race.

Chapter 5…Cultural Perceptions

Goal – SWBAT define the term 'Cultural Perception.'

Objective – Students will explain and gives examples about how they define the term 'Cultural Perception.'

Assessment –

1. In your own words, what is perception?

2. Give some examples of how the perception of one thing can be different across different cultures.

3. What is a genocide? Brown discusses two different genocides that have happened throughout history. Name them both.

4. Why do people feel more comfortable with people who are of the same color? Explain "strength in numbers"?

5. "Intentionality vs the intention." What do you think Brown means by this?

6. Consider the idea of transgenerational trauma from Chapter 4. How does this relate to the ideas Brown brings up in the first paragraph on page 66?

7. Brown discusses the serious water issue in Flint, Michigan. Considering the fact that not everyone in the U.S. has access to clean drinking water, do you believe that it is a right or a privilege to have access to clean drinking water? Discuss in groups.

8. Why do you think people are so willing to help children and families across the seas but not the people that live on the same soil as themselves?

9. Give some examples of stereotypes that you were taught growing up. How have your perceptions of these stereotypes changed? How have they stayed the same?

10. The *Pain Game* proves that pain is universal, regardless of how it is felt. As Brown states, it is something that is experienced by everyone. What are some other aspects of life that connect every person on this planet?

11. Bringing in the examples of Rosa Parks, the Underground Railroad, and the Boston Tea Party as well as any other examples you can think of, why is the line between right and wrong not always clear?

12. Why is it important for people to be held accountable for what they say?

13. What happens when people aren't held accountable for what they say? Can people say whatever they want without any repercussions? What happens if this occurs?

Activity – Play 'The Pain' Game.

Chapter 6...Indeed, Black Lives Truly Matter

Goal – SWBAT define in their own words what the term, 'Black Lives Matter' means to them individually.

Objective – Students will have a better understanding the mission and meaning of the Black Lives Matter group.

Assessment -

1. In this first paragraph of this chapter, Brown makes a short list of people who were victims of the violence brought on by the current social climate of the U.S. Using your own knowledge of current events, can you name any other victims from stories you have seen or heard on the news? Use the internet as a resource.

2. Why does saying All Lives Matter undermine the rights and change that the Black Lives Matter movement is fighting for?

3. Research the Black Panthers organization that was started in the 1960s. Read information about the group's history and goals while keeping in mind the social and political climate of the 1960s. Then, compare the Black Lives Matter movement with your knowledge of the Black Panthers. Lastly, contrast the Black Lives Matter movement with groups like the KKK.

4. Why is Blue Lives Matter so drastically different than Black Lives Matter?

5. "Black means to always be angry." Brown discusses this stereotype in this chapter. What are some other stereotypes that surround people who identify as Black?

6. Have you ever had a constant battle with either yourself or someone else where you consistently had to prove yourself because of a certain stereotype or perception that kept fighting its way to define you? If so, explain. If not, explain a stereotype that people have used to define you. How did it make you feel?

7. "It's always a roll of the dice and you have to play the hand that you've been dealt." In your own words, what does Brown mean by this?

8. What did Tamir Rice, Trayvon Martin, and Eric Garner all have in common? Make a list of similarities or explain in your own words. Use the internet as a resource to gain more information about their stories.

9. In your own opinion, what is a constructive yet meaningful way for people to protest in this country for them to positively enact change or even be heard by those with the ability to make positive change happen?

10. What do you believe defines a person of color?

11. To understand the Black community, it is important to be educated on the contributions many famous Black people have made, both in the past and present. Below is a list of influential Black people. Research and write what impact they have made on society:

Thurgood Marshall:

George Washington Carter:

Malcom X:

Huey P. Newton:

Jessie Williams:

Charlene Carruthers:

Chadwick Boseman:

Sage Steele:

Misty Copeland:

Activity–"Play the matters box."

Chapter 7...Cultural Differences

Goal – SWBAT define the terms, Cultural Differences, Ethnocentrism and Cultural Relativism.

Objective – Students will discuss what they have learned about other cultures different from their own.

Assessment –

1. Everyone has a culture or set of beliefs/norms that they identify with. What is one aspect of your culture that separates it from the cultures of other people?

2. What is something you have learned about another culture that is very different from your own culture? Compare and contrast the similarities and differences of what you learned to your own cultural experiences.

3. Define ethnocentrism and cultural relativism.

4. Brown says, "I also know that we all smile in the same language." Out of all the different cultures that you have encountered in your life, what are some connecting features that are consistent across different cultures?

5. In your own words, describe what qualities encompass a person who is globally minded? Why is it important to be a globally minded person?

6. Whether it is with your peers or colleagues, why is having cultural knowledge in the workplace and in the classroom necessary?

7. Read about Brown's trip to Mexico. As a person of color, specifically a Black man, do you think that the people of Mexico treated him similarly to the way people in the U.S. treat him? Think about people's cultural perceptions of people who are black in the U.S.

8. If you were playing *Ask Any Race Whatever Question You Want*, what questions would you have?

9. In your culture, how is mental illness treated? Do you agree with this? Why or why not?

10. Explain why an "us versus them" mentality is detrimental to our progress as a society.

11. Besides Christianity, what are some other religions that both white people and people of color practice? Make a list.

12. At the end of this chapter, Brown mentions a gray area between Black and White. What is your interpretation of this gray area?

13. What are some productive ways to bring people together to have developmental conversations about diversity?

Activity – Play 'Ask Any Race Whatever You Want' Game.

Chapter 8...Battle of the Genders

Goal – SWBAT define the term gender dichotomy.

Objective – Students will discuss how a person's gender role is shaped and perceived by others.

Assessment –

1. Define these terms:

Biological sex:

Gender identity:

Gender role:

Gender equality:

LGBTQIA:

2. Explain the gender dichotomy prevalent in our society? Why is believing in this dichotomy an inaccurate representation of how people identify on the gender spectrum.

3. Why is it important to be educated on the LGBTQIA community and the struggles/problems that they, as a minority, go through on a regular basis?

4. If you consider yourself a member of the LGBTQIA community, what are some of the struggles you have faced because of this? If you do not identify with this community, why is it important to become an ally?

5. Research ways you can educate yourself and others about the LGBTQIA community and how you can help. (i.e. Human Rights campaign, True Colors Fund, etc.)

6. In the game *Male or Female*, why were people's schemas of males and females so different?

7. Why is it important to understand that people's experiences shape which side they pick in *Male or Female* and that whatever side you pick there is no right or wrong answer?

8. Define privilege in terms of identifying as male or female. Does that privilege decrease with the amount of minority statuses a person identifies with? Explain why in your answer. (i.e. being a Black, Muslim woman)

9. Imagine you were playing *Male or Female*. What side would you pick for all the following categories: Intelligent, Violent, and Accommodating. Explain and justify your answer for each. Now, get into groups of four and explain your decisions to each member of the group.

10. List some examples of the ways that a person's gender role is shaped from the day they were born to present day.

11. Explain why it's essential that women empower other women. Why is it detrimental to knock other women down?

Activity – Play 'Male or Female' Game.

Chapter 9...Well This is Just a Woman's Issue

Goals – SWBAT define and list some woman's issues from experience and observation.

SWBAT define the term gender equality.

SWBAT define the term woman's suffrage.

Objective – Students will list how woman can be considered second to men and second in life experiences.

Assessment –

1. "Society makes it so that women are second-class citizens." List some areas of our society where women always fall second to men.

2. "Men need to be quieter on some issues that have nothing to do with them." What are some issues that have to do with women that are still largely dealt with by men?

3. In the second paragraph of this chapter, Brown makes a list of statements and questions that women hear on a daily basis. If you are a female, has anyone ever said anything similar to you? If so, how did it make you feel? If you are a male, have you ever said any of these words to a female? Whether your answer is yes or no, explain why saying these things can have a negative impact on a person.

4. List some double standards that women face in our society today.

5. Why is it important to educate the youth about rape and sexual assault, along with the sexual health education they receive in school?

6. Why is the way we educate women and men about rape wrong? How does this perpetuate rape culture even more?

7. Reflect on the previous discussions of stereotypes and perceptions. Why is it difficult for women to come forward about sexual assault, rape and/or abuse? Why is it difficult for men to come forward about sexual assault, rape and/or abuse?

8. Brown brings up the infamous Brock Turner case. Research this case. What was the story behind it, how was it dealt with and what was the verdict? Discuss in groups about what happened with this case. How does it make you feel? Explain.

9. How does the media oversexualize women? Give examples. Why is this a problem?

10. "No one can make you feel inferior without your consent." Eleanor Roosevelt said this. Explain this quote and what it means to you.

11. Why is it crucial to have women in the political sectors of our society? For example, think about policies affecting reproductive rights, health care, and the wage gap.

12. With regards to the Women's March in 2017, why was it important that there were people from all diverse backgrounds and genders supporting women?

13. Brown mentions terminology as one of the reasons that the perception of women is less than the perception of a man. Give some examples of this terminology.

14. Define women's suffrage.

15. "Limiting women's voices limits the possible outcomes." Explain this in your own words. Why is this an important concept to understand when thinking about gender equality?

Activity–Watch a video online about "Women's Suffrage."

Goal – SWBAT define the terms student affairs and multicultural competency.

Objective – Students will explain how they would make a university campus climate more inclusive and bridge the gap between academia, student affairs and students.

Assessment –

1. Like Brown, have you ever felt clueless about what you want to do with your life? If so, explain. If not, talk about what you want to pursue in your life.

2. Using your own experiences, why is it so difficult to enact change?

3. "The greatest resistance to change is fear." Interpret this in your own words.

4. In student affairs, why is inclusivity imperative?

5. Whether you are surrounded by peers or colleagues, how can you create an atmosphere of openness for the people that you surround yourself with? Why is this important?

6. Explain how an atmosphere of competition can be toxic for people who work together in the same field.

7. In student affairs, why is it important to get to know the people who you work with, both your colleagues and students, on a personal level? Is this applicable in fields outside of student affairs? Explain.

8. Why do some people see other people only for their skin color and not their qualifications? Is this wrong, or right? Explain.

9. How can invalidating the experiences and opinions of others be harmful to the workplace?

10. Imagine being in a resident director role at a university. How would your actions affect the way students view the institution?

11. "Relatability equals relationship and relationship equals growth in our students." What does Brown mean by this?

12. Define multicultural competency.

13. "Iron sharpens iron." Explain this quote in terms of constructive feedback.

14. What are some ways student affairs professionals can make a university campus climate more inclusive for everyone?

15. How can bridging the gap between academia and student affairs help improve the lives of the students at a university?

Activity–Discuss any improvements you would like to see in higher education.

Chapter 11…My Final Thoughts

Goal – SWBAT define the term 'Diversity Fluidity.'

Objective – Students will explain the term 'glass ceiling' and write a paragraph explaining if they are a 'dreamer' or a 'doer.'

Assessment –

1. "Diversity is fluid." Interpret this in your own words and explain what it means to you.

2. Brown says that his book is for anyone who wanted to learn something new. What are some things you learned from reading this book?

3. Brown talks about his parents being a very influential factor in his life. Who in your life has made an impact? What does this person mean to you?

4. Write down three things you want to accomplish within the next 30 days. Stick to a schedule a follow through on these goals.

5. Whether it is short term or long term, write down a dream of yours. Then, write down ways you can accomplish this dream.

6. Have you ever had your heart broken? Have you ever been in a situation where the problems you encountered were due to your empty pockets? Have you ever experienced failure? Pick one of these questions that relates to you and explain. How did your situation make you feel? How did you learn from it?

7. "Dreaming is free, but the hustle is sold separately." Explain what Brown means by this. How can you relate this quote to your own life?

8. Define the glass ceiling.

9. Why is creating your own sunshine extremely important?

10. Explain the balance between "always keep your guard up" and "wearing your heart on your sleeve"? Think about your past experiences and incorporate them into your response.

11. Recall a time in your life when you had to take responsibility for something that you did. How did it make you feel and what were the repercussions? Why is it important in life to take responsibility for your actions?

12. In terms of being religious or not being religious, what do you believe in? How does this affect the way you lead your life?

13. At the conclusion of his book, Brown emphasizes being the best version of yourself. What are some ways that you can improve yourself? Think about what you have learned from this book.

About the Author

Justin L. Brown is a renowned presenter and critically acclaimed speaker who has devoted his life to educating campuses, businesses, and society about cultural awareness. Justin helps to build the respect of others, communication, authentic relationships, and how to have a closer connection to God. After being fed up with the world and its continuing decline of respect, morals, and values, Justin was determined to make a difference. Justin's passion is for working with students developed while pursuing a bachelor's degree in public relations from Slippery Rock University. During his undergraduate tenure, Justin was actively involved on campus through working and collaborating with various offices and departments. It was during this time that Justin created the Diversity Awareness Program (D.A.P.), a program dedicated to raising awareness and educating college campuses about the importance of diversity and embracing all cultures and backgrounds. Justin then continued nurturing D.A.P. through his graduate studies at the Indiana University of Pennsylvania, while working towards earning his master's degree in Student Affairs in Higher Education. D.A.P. has successfully grown in popularity, having visited over 400 colleges and universities and established over 20 chapters within those institutions. For a while, parents, friends, and professors had been asking Justin to put his ideas and concepts into a book that everyone could use and learn from. This book is the product of that demand.

About Diversity Awareness Program

The purpose of D.A.P. is to encourage diversity and cultural unity in all areas of life among students, faculty, and staff on a university campus. This will be accomplished through energetic and vigorous engagements and dynamic discussions on issues and ideas. D.A.P. will serve as a catalyst in encouraging students and community members to search for opportunities to become more culturally aware and conscious.

This organization has educated students around the country by inviting a diverse group of people together to participate in activities that not only help them to know each other in small groups, but also to have discussion topics as a large group.

The energy and commitment of the collective whole of its membership is amazingly strong. It has approximately over 50,000 members meeting weekly; voluntarily coming together to discuss, role play, and challenge each other on social issues, ideas, personal relationships, stereotypes, cultural identities, and so much more.

If you would like to donate to the Diversity Awareness Program Scholarship Fund, please contact Justin directly.

If interested in the program, please view our website.

http://diversityawareness.wix.com/program

To schedule Justin for a keynote speech, assembly, convocation, seminar, workshop, educational convention or training session, please contact:

Justin L. Brown
40 Lauren Lane
Coatesville Pa, 19320

Justin will customize and format any program to fit the needs and expectations of the organization or audience.

Contact Justin directly: **Email:** justinbrown331@gmail.com

Published By
Books Speak For You
Publishing House
1-800-757-0598
Booksspeakforyou.com

Made in the USA
Coppell, TX
07 June 2021